To Boon - My partner in all journeys.

Copyright © 2020 by Michael Harrigan
All rights reserved. This book or any portion thereof may not be reproduced or used in any manner whatsoever without the express written permission of the publisher except for the use of brief quotations in a book review or scholarly journal.

First Printing: 2020
ISBN 978-1-910567-08-1

Michael Harrigan Designs
88/9 Chakrapong Road, Banglumpoo
Bangkok 10200 Thailand

www.thismanknits.com

Published in 2020 by Anchor and Bee
www.anchorandbee.com

Travel-inspired Knits

10 Original Patterns for Hand Knit Accessories

by Michael Harrigan

About The Collection

The 10 patterns in this book represent a collection of some of my all-time favorites, with designs ranging from simple stranded colorwork to textured patterns and eyelet lace. They are all suitable for intermediate-level knitters.

My inspiration comes from my travels around the world. I like to spend time in historic settings, visiting local artisan markets and bazaars, and also taking in landscapes and natural features. I try to recreate what I have seen in stitch patterns – interpreting elements of nature, landmarks, and textiles I've come across.

You'll find triangular shawls and shawlettes, knit from the top down and the bottom up; easy-to-knit stranded colorwork cowls; a Fair Isle scarf knit in the round (and a couple of Fair Isle beanies); and a winter holiday-themed shawl that combines a few different colorwork techniques.

Photo: The view from where I knit – at home on the Gulf of Thailand

About Me

When I was around nine years old my mother showed me the basics of knitting and crocheting. However, I grew up on a farm in the northeastern US, and in that area and at that time, knitting was not one of the approved pastimes for a young boy. The needles and crochet hooks were put aside – for quite a few years, in fact.

Several years ago I started to knit again and it quickly became an integral part of my daily life. I bought lots of books and learned a wide range of techniques. Then I bought more books and experimented with lace, texture, and colorwork stitch patterns. It wasn't long before I started combining stitch patterns into designs and decided to write out the instructions so I could share them with others (and remember them). I soon discovered I could upload the patterns to the internet and was off on a new adventure. I also improved my skills and increased my range through the Master Hand Knitter certification program of The Knitting Guild Association (tkga.org).

Over the past few years I have designed patterns for accessories, including shawls, wraps, cowls, hats – and a Fair Isle-patterned gansey. I've self-published the majority of my designs but have also produced others for yarn companies and online and print magazines.

My work has been influenced by Kaffe Fassett's creativity with color. Overall, I'm most inspired by the historic traditions of Shetland and the stitch patterns of Fair Isle and of the Baltic and Scandinavian countries – and the countless knitters over the centuries who have contributed to that body of work.

Travel has a major impact on both the motifs and colors I use in my designs. Some decades ago I spent the better part of a year in Central America and was captivated by the colorful work of artisans in Mexico and Guatemala. Many years later my travels took me to Africa, where I was enthralled by the magic and mystery of Egypt and Morocco and the talented artisans of South Africa. I have been fascinated by the designs of rugs in Turkey and the embroidery I've come across in China. There's such an amazing wealth of hand-crafted riches throughout the world – and I certainly enjoy travels of discovery.

A couple of summers ago, we visited the Shetland Islands – long an inspiration to me, both for the knitted lace from the northern island of Unst, and the wonderfully colorful patterns of Fair Isle. On a trip to Estonia, Latvia, and Lithuania last year I had the opportunity to get some hands-on advice on color-stranding knitting technique in Riga, Latvia. At the end of that trip, on a visit to the Russian National Museum in St. Petersburg, I found inspiration for a new colorwork design based on a piece of ethnic embroidery.

Since I moved to Thailand in late 1998, the country's natural environment, iconic images, and architecture have provided ongoing inspiration for my designs.

I hope you enjoy knitting these patterns!

Michael Harrigan

Bangkok, Thailand

https://www.ravelry.com/designers/michael-harrigan

www.thismanknits.com

Contents

Page

Twists and Turns Bandana Shawlette   1

Inspired a by a transection of geometric shapes that reflect the interplay of shadows and light, as seen on the pavement from a seaside cafe in Croatia

Vertical Fair Isle Cowl   9

Traditional Fair Isle stitch patterns are featured in a design that has a unique focus on vertical pattern placement

Ultra Fair Isle Beanies   13

Shetland's tiny Fair Isle produced a treasure trove of stitch patterns over time and a few of my favorites are incorporated into this design, which is the same for both hats (the distribution of color creates the difference)

Fair Isle Scarf in Blues and Greys   19

Continuing with the Fair Isle tradition, this is the third in my trio of designs inspired by the islands far off the northern coast of Scotland. Knit in the round, this scarf is reversible

Embroidery-Inspired Colorwork Cowl   23

Kargopol (Russia) embroidery seen in St. Petersburg's Russian Museum is the source of this stitch pattern

Page

PawPrints Shawlette 27

Cat footprints on the car windscreen during a trip to France are the back story to this design

Sea Changes Shawl 33

From where I knit, I am fortunate to have a lovely view of the sea and am fascinated by the changes to its surface throughout the day: this triangular shawl is my interpretation

Northern Leaves Triangular Scarf 43

Autumn leaves are captured in a pattern that features a Shetland leaf stitch pattern and an Estonian leaf motif

Winter Holiday Shawl 51

This colorful accessory captures the Christmas spirit, featuring snowflakes and candy canes

Estonian Colorwork Cowl 61

A stitch pattern found in an old publication in a Tallinn thrift shop forms the basis for this piece

Twists and Turns

STOCKINETTE AND LACE KNIT BANDANA

This triangular-shaped shawl is worked in stockinette stitch and features a vertical zigzag lace panel intersected by left and right-side chevron lace panels.

Measurements: 47x14" / 119.5x35.5cm after blocking

Gauge: 30sts x 48 rows = 4"/10cm in Stockinette stitch pattern

What you'll need:

Malabrigo MECHITA (100g, 420yds, 100% Superwash Merino Wool): 1 skein Sirenas

US size 2 (2.75mm) needles or size needed to obtain gauge

1 stitch marker

Tapestry needle

Abbreviations
Sskpo – Ssk, then place stitch back on left needle. Lift second stitch on left needle over ssk loop, then return ssk loop to right needle.

Stitch patterns

Zigzag Lace Stitch Pattern (mult of 16 sts)

See chart.

Row 1: K2, (yo, ssk) 5 times, k4.

Row 2 and all WS rows: Purl.

Row 3: K3, (yo, ssk) 5 times, k3.

Twists and Turns

Row 5: K4, (yo, ssk) 5 times, k2.

Row 7: K5, (yo, ssk) 5 times, k1.

Row 9: K6, (yo, ssk) 5 times.

Row 11: K4, (k2tog, yo) 5 times, k2.

Row 13: K3, (k2tog, yo) 5 times, k3.

Row 15: K2, (k2tog, yo) 5 times, k4.

Row 17: K1, (k2tog, yo) 5 times, k5.

Row 19: (K2tog, yo) 5 times, k6.

Row 20: Purl.

Repeat 20 rows for pattern.

Chevron Lace Stitch Pattern – RIGHT (mult of 12 sts)

See chart.

Row 1: K1, yo, ssk, k7, k2tog, yo.

Row 2 and all WS rows: Purl.

Row 3: (Yo, ssk) twice, k5, k2tog, yo, k1.

Row 5: K1, (yo, ssk) twice, k3, (k2tog, yo) twice.

Row 7: (Yo, ssk) 3 times, k1, (k2tog, yo) twice, k1.

Row 9: K1, (yo, ssk) twice, yo, sskpo, yo, (k2tog, yo) twice.

Row 11: K2, (yo, ssk) twice, yo, sskpo, yo, k2tog, yo, k1.

Row 13: K3, (yo, ssk) twice, yo, sskpo, yo, k2.

Row 15: K4, yo, ssk, yo, sskpo, yo, k3.

Row 17: K5, yo, sskpo, yo, k4.

Row 19: K6, yo, ssk, k4.

Row 20: Purl.

Chevron Lace Stitch Pattern – LEFT (mult of 12 sts)

See chart.

Row 1: Yo, ssk, k7, k2tog, yo, k1.

Row 2 and all WS rows: Purl.

Row 3: K1, yo, ssk, k5, (k2tog, yo) twice.

Row 5: (Yo, ssk) twice, k3, (k2tog, yo) twice, k1.

Row 7: K1, (yo, ssk) twice, k1, (k2tog, yo) 3 times.

Row 9: (Yo, ssk) twice, yo, sskpo, yo, (k2tog, yo) twice, k1.

Row 11: K1, yo, ssk, yo, sskpo, yo, (k2tog, yo) twice, k2.

Row 13: K2, yo, sskpo, yo, (k2tog, yo) twice, k3.

Row 15: K3, yo, sskpo, yo, k2tog, yo, k4.

Row 17: K4, yo, sskpo, yo, k5.

Row 19: K4, k2tog, yo, k6.

Row 20: Purl.

CO 18 sts

Set-up

Row 1 (RS): K1, yo, k16, yo, k1. (20 sts)

Row 2 (WS): Knit.

Row 3: (K1, yo) twice, k16, (yo, k1) twice. (24 sts)

Row 4: Knit.

Row 5: (K1, yo) twice, k2, yo, place marker, k16, yo, k2, (yo, k1) twice. (30 sts)

Row 6: K2, p26, k2.

Twists and Turns

Section A

Row 7: (K1, yo) twice, knit to marker, yo, sm, work Row 1 of Zigzag Lace Pattern, yo, knit to last 2 sts, (yo, k1) twice. (36 sts)

Row 8 and all WS rows: K4, purl to last 4 sts, k4.

Row 9: (K1, yo) twice, knit to marker, yo, sm, work Row 3 of Zigzag Lace Pattern, yo, knit to last 2 sts, (yo, k1) twice. (42 sts)

Row 11: (K1, yo) twice, knit to marker, yo, sm, work Row 5 of Zigzag Lace Pattern, yo, knit to last 2 sts, (yo, k1) twice. (48 sts)

Row 13: (K1, yo) twice, knit to marker, yo, sm, work Row 7 of Zigzag Lace Pattern, yo, knit to last 2 sts, (yo, k1) twice. (54 sts)

Row 15: (K1, yo) twice, knit to marker, yo, sm, work Row 9 of Zigzag Lace Pattern, yo, knit to last 2 sts, (yo, k1) twice. (60 sts)

Row 17: (K1, yo) twice, knit to marker, yo, sm, work Row 11 of Zigzag Lace Pattern, yo, knit to last 2 sts, (yo, k1) twice. (66 sts)

Row 19: (K1, yo) twice, knit to marker, yo, sm, work Row 13 of Zigzag Lace Pattern, yo, knit to last 2 sts, (yo, k1) twice. (72 sts)

Row 21: (K1, yo) twice, knit to marker, yo, sm, work Row 15 of Zigzag Lace Pattern, yo, knit to last 2 sts, (yo, k1) twice. (78 sts)

Row 23: (K1, yo) twice, knit to marker, yo, sm, work Row 17 of Zigzag Lace Pattern, yo, knit to last 2 sts, (yo, k1) twice. (84 sts)

Row 25: (K1, yo) twice, knit to marker, yo, sm, work Row 19 of Zigzag Lace Pattern, yo, knit to last 2 sts, (yo, k1) twice. (90 sts)

Row 26: K4, purl to last 4 sts, k4.

Repeat Rows 7-26 three times. (270 sts)

Section B

Row 1: (K1, yo) twice, k2tog, yo, (work Row 1 of Chevron Lace Pattern-R) 10 times, k3, yo, sm, work Row 1 of Zigzag Lace Pattern, yo, k3, (work Row 1 of Chevron Lace Pattern-L) 10 times, yo, ssk, (yo, k1) twice. (276 sts)

Row 2 and all WS rows: K4, purl to last 4 sts, k4.

Row 3: (K1, yo) twice, k1, k2tog, yo, k1, (work Row 3 of Chevron Lace Pattern-R) 10 times, yo, ssk, k2, yo, sm, work Row 3 of Zigzag Lace Pattern, yo, k2, k2tog, yo, (work Row 3 of Chevron Lace Pattern-L) 10 times, k1, yo, ssk, k1, (yo, k1) twice. (282 sts)

Row 5: (K1, yo) twice, k2, (k2tog, yo) twice, (work Row 5 of Chevron Lace Pattern-R) 10 times, k1, yo, ssk, k2, yo, sm, work Row 5 of Zigzag Lace Pattern, yo, k2, k2tog, yo, k1, (work Row 5 of Chevron Lace Pattern-L) 10 times, (yo, ssk) twice, k2, (yo, k1) twice. (288 sts)

Row 7: (K1, yo) twice, k3, (k2tog, yo) twice, k1, (work Row 7 of Chevron Lace Pattern-R) 10 times, (yo, ssk) twice, k2, yo, sm, work Row 7 of Zigzag Lace Pattern, yo, k2, (k2tog, yo) twice, (work Row 7 of Chevron Lace Pattern-L) 10 times, k1, (yo, ssk) twice, k3, (yo, k1) twice. (294 sts)

Row 9: (K1, yo) twice, k1, yo, ssk, yo, sskpo, yo, (k2tog, yo) twice, (work Row 9 of Chevron Lace Pattern-R) 10 times, k1, (yo, ssk) twice, k2, yo, sm, work Row 9 of Zigzag Lace Pattern, yo, k2, (k2tog, yo) twice, k1, (work Row 9 of Chevron Lace Pattern-L) 10 times, (yo, ssk) twice, yo, sskpo, yo, k2tog, yo, k1, (yo, k1) twice. (300 sts)

Row 11: (K1, yo) twice, k2, (yo, ssk) twice, yo, sskpo, yo, k2tog, yo, k1, (work Row 11 of Chevron Lace Pattern-R) 10 times, k2, (yo, ssk) twice, k2, yo, sm, work Row 11 of Zigzag Lace Pattern, yo, k2, (k2tog, yo) twice, k2, (work Row 11 of Chevron Lace Pattern-L) 10 times, k1, yo, k2tog, yo, sskpo, yo, (k2tog, yo) twice, k2, (yo, k1) twice. (306 sts)

Row 13: (K1, yo) twice, k5, (yo, ssk) twice, yo, sskpo, yo, k2, (work Row 13 of Chevron Lace Pattern-R) 10 times, k3, (yo, ssk) twice, k2, yo, sm, work Row 13 of Zigzag Lace Pattern, yo, k2, (k2tog, yo) twice, k3, (work Row 13 of Chevron Lace Pattern-L) 10 times, k2, yo, sskpo, yo, (k2tog, yo) twice, k5, (yo, k1) twice. (312 sts)

Row 15: (K1, yo) twice, k8, yo, ssk, yo, sskpo, yo, k3, (work Row 15 of Chevron Lace Pattern-R) 10 times, k4, (yo, ssk) twice, k2, yo, sm, work Row 15 of Zigzag Lace Pattern, yo, k2, (k2tog, yo)

Twists and Turns

twice, k4, (work Row 15 of Chevron Lace Pattern-L) 10 times, k3, yo, sskpo, yo, k2tog, yo, k8, (yo, k1) twice. (318 sts)

Row 17: (K1, yo) twice, k11, yo, sskpo, yo, k4, (work Row 17 of Chevron Lace Pattern-R) 10 times, k5, (yo, ssk) twice, k2, yo, sm, work Row 17 of Zigzag Lace Pattern, yo, k2, (k2tog, yo) twice, k5, (work Row 17 of Chevron Lace Pattern-L) 10 times, k4, yo, sskpo, yo, k11, (yo, k1) twice. (324 sts)

Row 19: (K1, yo) twice, k2, yo, ssk, k10, yo, ssk, k4, (work Row 19 of Chevron Lace Pattern-R) 10 times, k6, (yo, ssk) twice, k2, yo, sm, work Row 19 of Zigzag Lace Pattern, yo, k2, (k2tog, yo) twice, k6, (work Row 17 of Chevron Lace Pattern-L) 10 times, k4, k2tog, yo, k10, k2tog, yo, k2, (yo, k1) twice. (330 sts)

Row 20: K4, purl to last 4 sts, k4.

Section C

Repeat Rows 7-26 of Section A once. (390 sts)

Next row (RS): (K1, yo) twice, (k2tog, yo) 92 times, k1, rm, yo, k16, yo, (k2tog, yo) 92 times, k1, (yo, ssk) twice. (396 sts)

Next row (WS): Knit

Bind off loosely.

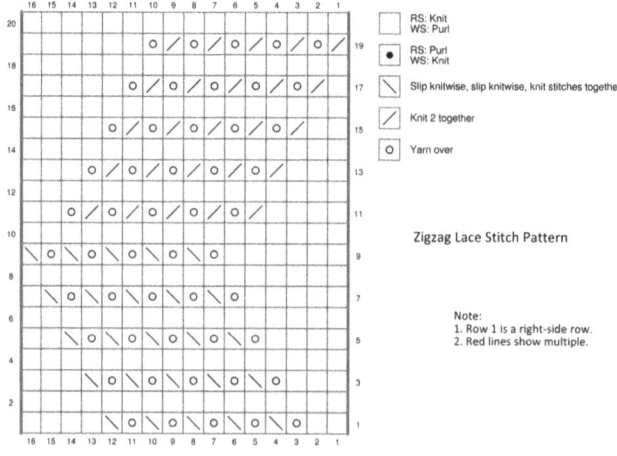

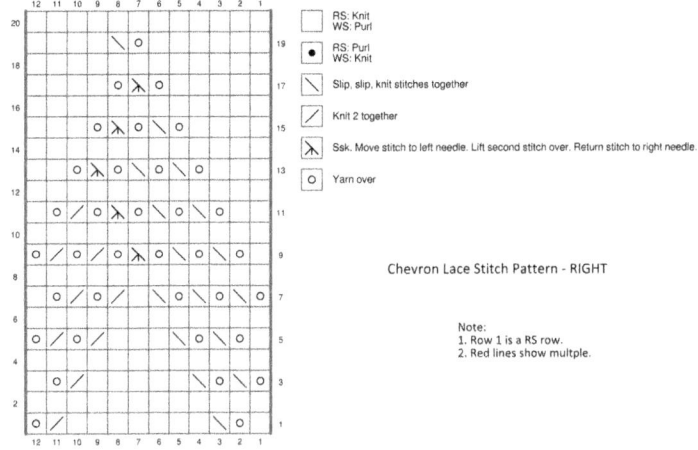

Chevron Lace Stitch Pattern - RIGHT

Note:
1. Row 1 is a RS row.
2. Red lines show multple.

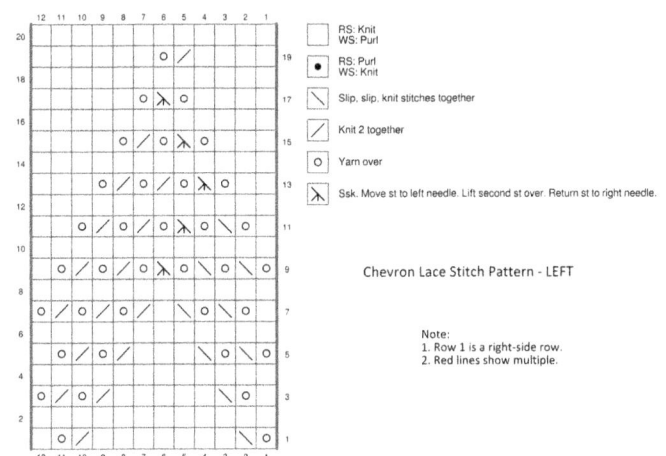

Chevron Lace Stitch Pattern - LEFT

Note:
1. Row 1 is a right-side row.
2. Red lines show multiple.

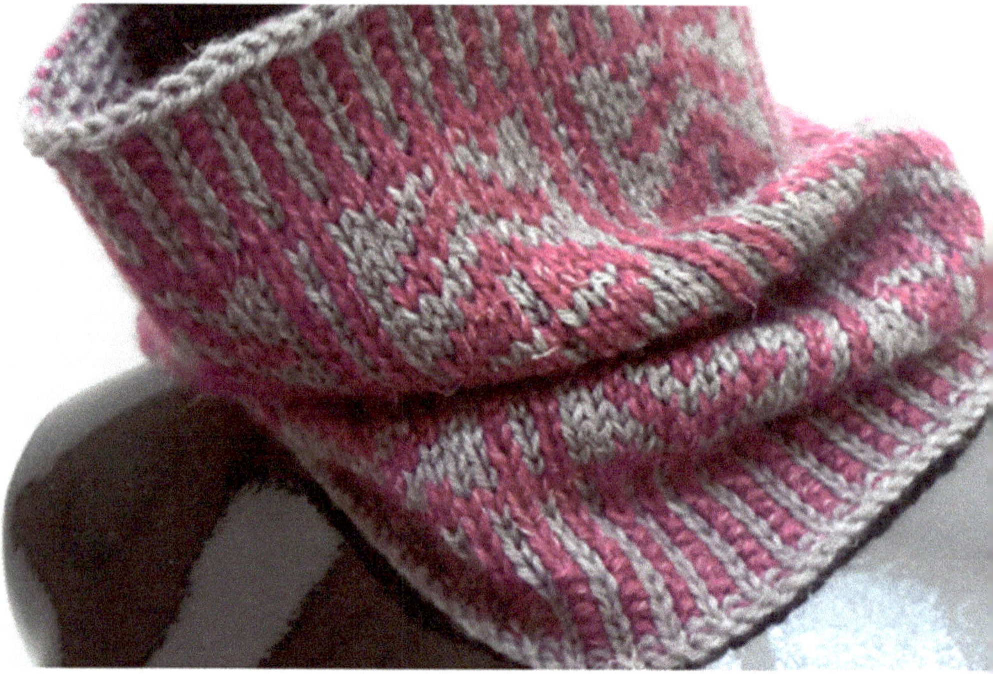
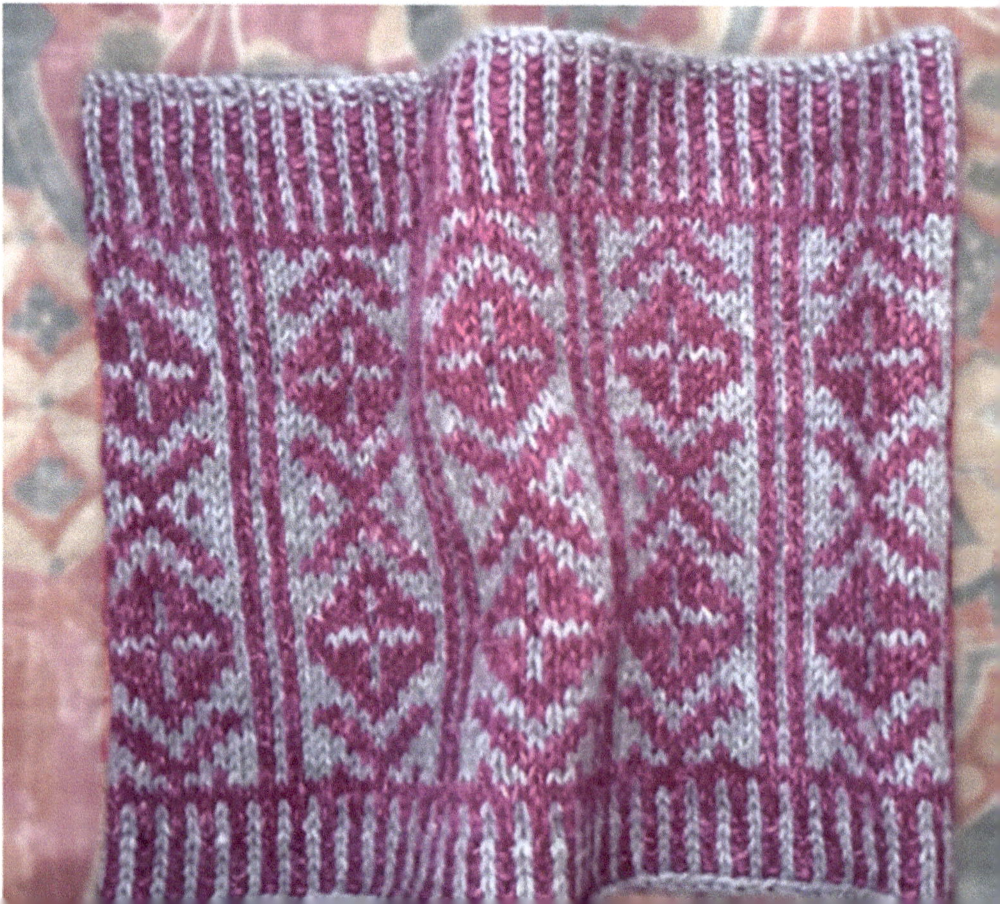

Vertical Fair Isle Cowl

FAIR ISLE COWL

This cowl / neck warmer features a vertical Fair Isle color pattern and is knit in the round. Two colors of Stolen Stitches Nua Worsted (Kitten Fluff and Cafe Flamingo) form the pattern. This is a suitable project for someone relatively new to color stranded knitting, as only two colors are involved throughout.

Measurements: Circumference: 21" / 53cm. Height: 9.5" / 24cm

Gauge: In Fair Isle stitch pattern, 24 sts & 24 rnds = 4"/10cm.

What you'll need:

Stolen Stitches NUA WORSTED (50g, 100m/109yds, 60% Merino Wool/20% Yak/20% Linen): 1 skein each of Kitten Fluff (Color A) and Cafe Flamingo (Color B)

US size 7 (4.5mm) 16" (40cm) circular needle or size needed to obtain gauge

Stitch marker

Tapestry needle

Cast on 126 stitches in Color A. Join in round, placing stitch marker to indicate beginning of round.

Work 9 multiples of the 29 rows of Chart 1 on the 126 stitches.

Work 9 multiples of the 28 rows of Chart 2 on the 126 stitches.

BO loosely in Color A. Weave in ends and block to measurements.

Vertical Fair Isle Cowl

Note

1. Charts are worked in the round.
2. Green lines show 14-stitch multiple: 9 multiples are worked per round.

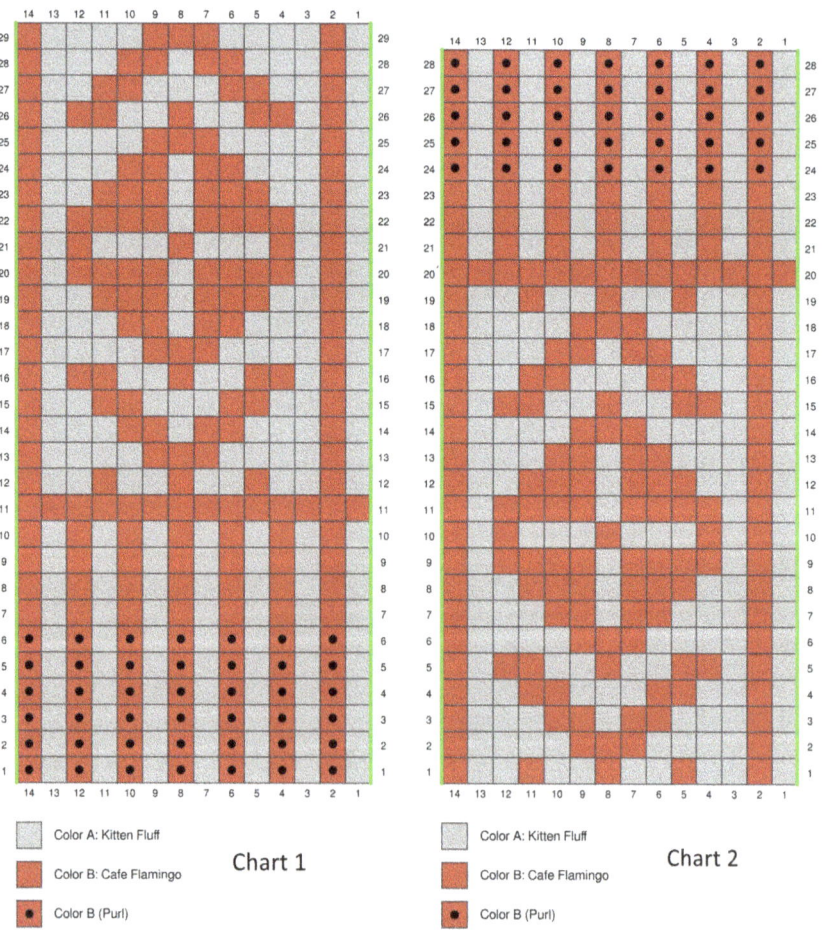

Ultra Fair Isle Beanies

FAIR ISLE HAT

This hat features traditional Fair Isle patterns and is knit in the round. The design for both hats is the same: the distribution of colors is different. Separate directions follow for the two hats.

Measurements: Circumference (unstretched): 20in/51cm
Height: 7-1/2 in/19cm

Gauge: 32 sts and 36 rows = 4 in/10cm in Fair Isle pattern

What you'll need:

Jamieson's of Shetland ULTRA (25g/194m; 100% Shetland Wool) 1 skein each #103 Sholmit (Light Grey); #102 Shaela (Dark Grey); #303 Seascape (Light Blue); #168 Clyde Blue (Dark Blue); and #527 Lava (Red)

US3/3.25mm 16in/40cm circular needle or size needed to obtain gauge

US3/3.25mm double-pointed needles or size needed to obtain gauge

Stitch marker

Tapestry needle

Directions for Hat #1 (right side of top featured photo)

Brim

CO 160 sts with Dark Blue. Join in round and place marker to indicate beginning of round.

Work 8 rounds in k1, p1 corrugated ribbing (Dark Blue for knit sts; Dark Grey for purl sts)

Ultra Fair Isle Beanies

Body

Knit 1 round in Dark Blue.

Work next round as follows: *K1 (Dark Blue), k1 (Light Blue); rep from * to end.

Knit 1 round in Light Blue.

Work 16 multiples of the 4 rounds of Chart 1, with Light Blue as the background color and Dark Grey as the design color (design color is shown in Black on chart).

Knit 1 round in Light Blue.

Knit 1 round in Light Grey.

Work 16 multiples of the 11 rounds of Chart 2, with Light Grey as the background color and Dark Grey as the design color (design color is shown in Black on chart). For Round 6, change the design color to Red – for that round only.

Knit 2 rounds in Light Grey.

Work 16 multiples of the 9 rounds of Chart 3, with Light Grey as the background color and Dark Blue as the design color.

Knit 2 rounds in Light Grey, decreasing 4 sts evenly on the second round. (156 sts)

Crown

Work 12 multiples of the 23 rounds of Chart 4A, following the color designations on the chart.

Thread a tapestry needle and run the yarn through the final 12 sts. Pull tight and weave in the yarn end.

Finishing

Weave in ends. Block to dimensions.

Directions for Hat #2 (left side of top featured photo)

Brim

CO 160 sts with Red. Join in round and place marker to indicate beginning of round.

Work 8 rounds in k1, p1 corrugated ribbing (Red for knit sts; Dark Grey for purl sts)

Body

Knit 1 round in Red.

Work next round as follows: *K1 (Red), k1 (Dark Blue); rep from * to end.

Knit 1 round in Dark Blue.

Work 16 multiples of the 4 rounds of Chart 1, with Light Grey as the background color and Dark Grey as the design color (design color is shown in Black on chart)

Knit 1 round in Light Grey.

Knit 1 round in Dark Blue.

Work 16 multiples of the 11 rounds of Chart 2, with Dark Blue as the background color and Red as the design color (design color is shown in Black on chart). For Round 6, change the design color to Light Blue – for that round only.

Knit 2 rounds in Dark Blue.

Work 16 multiples of the 9 rounds of Chart 3, with Red as the background color and Light Grey as the design color.

Knit 2 rounds in Dark Grey, decreasing 4 sts evenly on the second round. (156 sts)

Crown

Work 12 multiples of the 23 rounds of Chart 4B, following the color designations on the chart.

Thread a tapestry needle and run the yarn through the final 12 sts.

Ultra Fair Isle Beanies

Pull tight and weave in the yarn end.

Finishing

Weave in ends. Block to dimensions.

Note
1. Worked in the round
2. Red lines show multiple

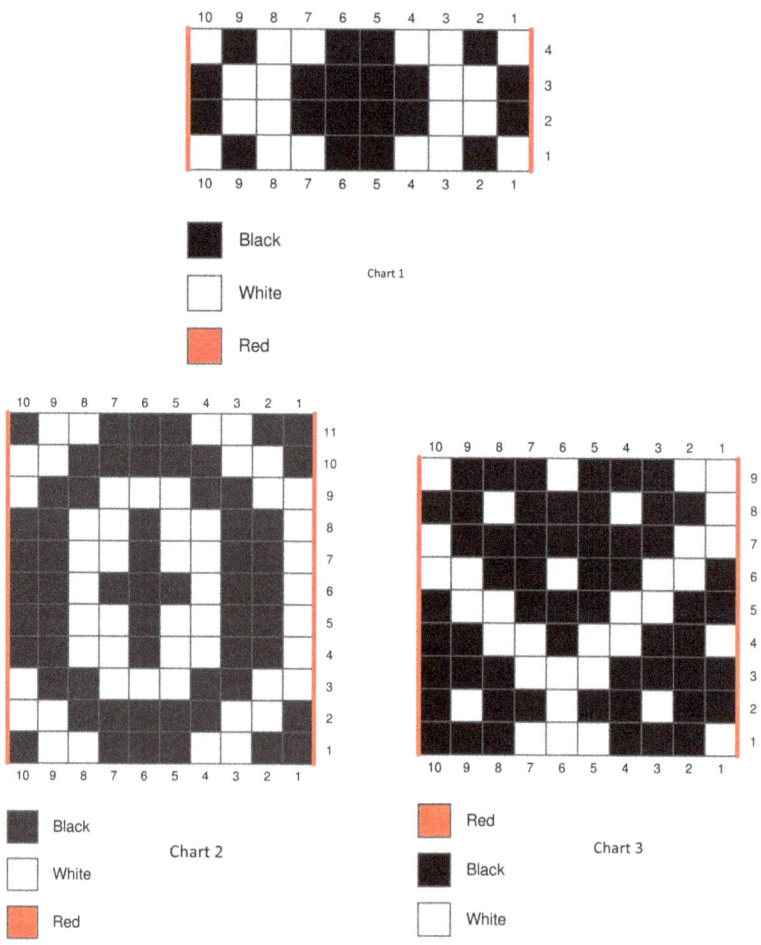

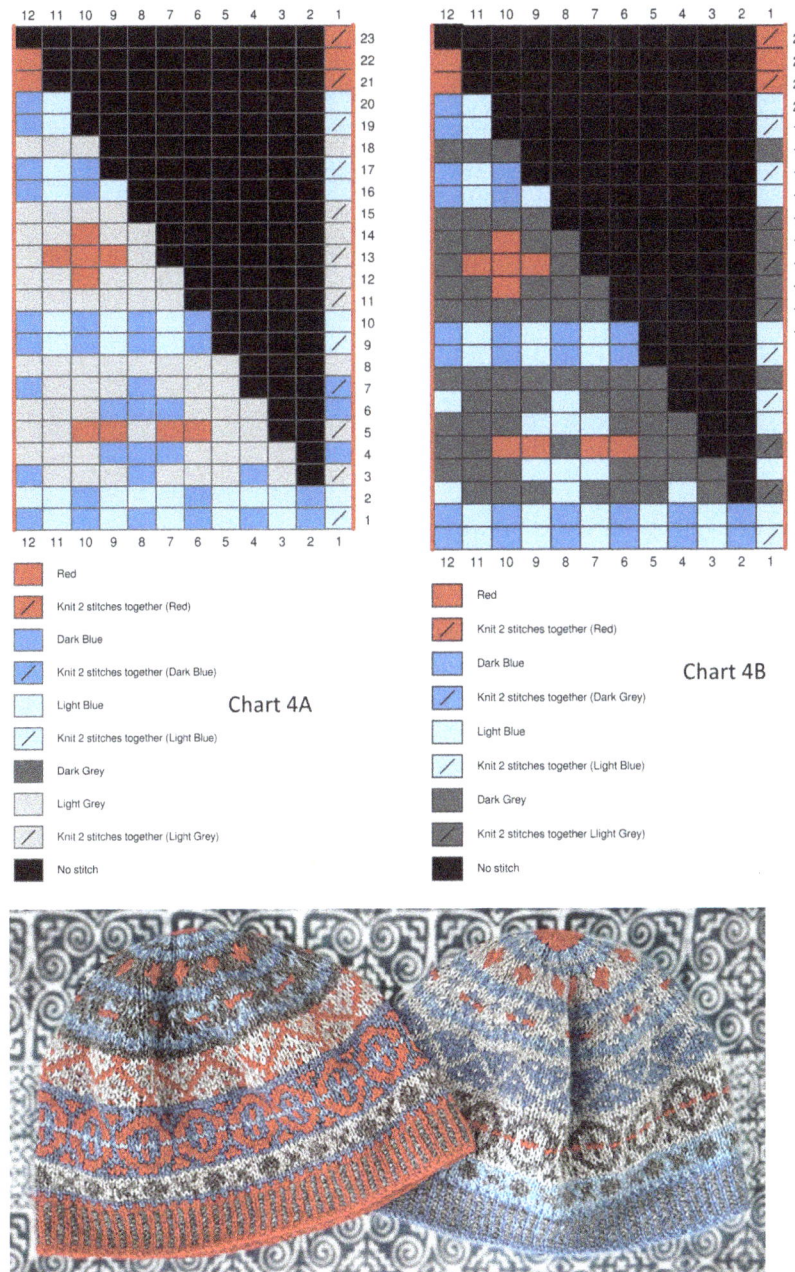

Fair Isle-Patterned Scarf in Blues and Greys

KNIT IN THE ROUND, REVERSIBLE

The scarf is worked in the round on a 16" (40cm) needle. The bind off used is a 3-Needle Bind-off that seams the final end. The piece is then turned inside out, the yarn tails woven in, and then the piece is turned right-side out. At the cast-on edge, stitches are picked up and knit and then the 3-Needle Bind-off is used to close that end.

Measurements: 6.5x72 inches (16.5x183cm)

Gauge: Over Fair Isle Chart, 31 sts & 38 rounds = 4"/10cm.

What you'll need:

Jamieson's ULTRA (0.9 ounces/25 grams, 212 yards/194 meters, 50% Shetland wool/50% lambswool): 3 balls #103 Sholmit (color A); 3 balls #168 Clyde Blue (color B); 2 balls #102 Shaela (color C); 2 balls #330 Seascape (color D); and 1 ball #572 Lava (color E)

Size 3 (3.25mm) 16" (40cm) circular needle – or size needed to obtain gauge

Size 3 (3.25mm) single needle (for 3-needle bind-off)

Stitch marker

Tapestry needle

For a short tutorial on how to work the 3-Needle Bind-off see http://knitty.com/ISSUEfall06/FEATfall06TT.html

(Note that for this scarf, the right sides are facing out during the bind-off, and the stitches are divided so that there are 51 on each side of the circular needle).

Fair Isle-Patterned Scarf in Blues and Greys

CO 102 sts. Join in round, placing stitch marker at beg of round.

Work sections in the Fair Isle Stitch Pattern as follows *(see chart)*:

Section 1: With colors A and B work the 51-stitch repeat twice on each round for 61 rounds (from Round 1 to Round 61).

Section 2: With colors A and B work the 51-stitch repeat twice on each round for 61 rounds (from Round 61 to Round 1).

Section 3: With colors C and D work the 51-stitch repeat twice on each round for 61 rounds (from Round 1 to Round 61).

Section 4: With colors C and D work the 51-stitch repeat twice on each round for 61 rounds (from Round 61 to Round 1).

Section 5 and Section 6: Repeat Section 1 and Section 2. Change to color E to work the last round of Section 6.

Section 7 and Section 8: Repeat Section 2 and Section 1. Work the first round of Section 7 in color E.

Section 9 and Section 10: Repeat Section 3 and Section 4.

Next row: Change to color E and knit across round.

BO in color E using 3-Needle Bind-off technique.

Finishing

Turn inside out and weave in yarn tails. Turn right-side out and, using color E, pick up 102 stitches along cast-on edge. Knit 1 round. Work 3-Needle Bind-off on cast-on end. Wet block to finished measurements.

Note that color A becomes color C and color B becomes color D in Sections 3, 4, 9, and 10.

Embroidery Inspired Fair Isle Neck Warmer
KNIT IN THE ROUND

Stranded colorwork inspired by an ethnic Russian embroidery pattern.

Measurements: 19.5x9.5 inches (49.5x24.1 cm)

Gauge: Over Fair Isle Chart, 30 sts & 36 rounds = 4"/10cm.

What you'll need:

Jamieson's of Shetland SPINDRIFT (25 grams, 105 meters, 100% pure Shetland wool): 2 balls each of #688 (Mermaid – Color A); #182 (Buttercup – Color B) – or any other yarn that will yield the gauge indicated

3mm 40cm circular needle – or size needed to obtain gauge

Stitch marker

Tapestry needle

CO 144 sts using Color A and the Cable Cast On* method. Join and place a stitch marker at the beginning of the round.

*For instructions on how to work this technique see https://www.loveknitting.com/how-to-work-cable-cast-on

Knit one round in Color A.

Work the 85 rounds of the Embroidery Inspired Fair Isle Stitch Pattern chart (2 multiples of each round).

BO in Color B.

Finishing

Turn inside out and weave in yarn tails. Wet block to finished

Embroidery Inspired Fair Isle Neck Warmer

measurements.

Note
Work in rounds, starting at the lower right. Each round of the pattern multiple (72 sts) is worked twice.

PawPrints

SHAWLETTE WITH TASSEL

This bandana / shawlette is knit from the bottom point up, with increases worked at the edges of all right-side rows. The central panel and topline feature a traditional Shetland Cat's Paw eyelet pattern. An optional, decorative tassel is attached to the bottom point after blocking.

Measurements: Wingspan: 40" Height: 20"

Gauge: In Garter stitch, 20 sts & 48 rows = 4"/10cm.

What you'll need:

Eden Cottage Yarns HAYTON 4-PLY (100g, 350m, 80% Merino; 10% Cashmere; 10% Nylon): 1 skein each of Briar Rose (Color A) and Cosmos Flowerbed (Color B)

US size 4 (3.5mm) 32" (80cm) circular needle or size needed to obtain gauge

Two stitch markers

Tapestry needle

Abbreviations
PM	place marker
SM	slip marker
k2tog	knit 2 stitches together
skp	slip 1 stitch, knit the next stitch, pass the slipped stitch over the knit stitch
sk2p	slip 1 stitch, knit the next 2 stitches together, pass the slipped stitch over
yo	yarn over

Cat's Paw Stitch Pattern

See chart - (multiple of 7 stitches)

PawPrints

Row 1: K1, k2tog, yo, k1, yo, skp, k1.

Row 2 and all other wrong-side rows: Knit.

Row 3: K2tog, yo, k3, yo, skp.

Row 5: K2, yo, sk2p, yo, k2.

Rows 7 and 9: Knit.

Row 10: Knit

Repeat Rows 1-10 for pattern.

Cast on 3 stitches with Color A.

Knit one row and continue as follows:

Row 1: K1, yo, k1, yo, k1.

Row 2 and all wrong-side rows throughout: Knit.

Row 3: K1, yo, k3, yo, k1.

Row 5: K1, yo, k5, yo, k1.

Row 7: K1, yo, pm, k7, pm, yo, k1.

Row 8: Knit.

Work in pattern as established, slipping markers on both sides of the 7 central stitches, until you have 21 stitches on your needles, ending with a wrong-side row.

Continue working the beginning and ending increases and work a total of 16 repeats of the 10-row Cat's Paw stitch pattern on the center 7 stitches. (181 sts)

Work one more 10-row pattern repeat, changing to Color B at the beginning of Row 7. Remove markers on the last row.

Next, work the Cat's Paw stitch pattern across entire rows as follows:

Row 1: K1, yo, k1, pm, (work Row 1 of Cat's Paw pattern, k3) 18 times; work Row 1 of Cat's Paw pattern, pm, k1, yo, k1.

Row 2 and all wrong-side rows: Knit.

Rows 3, 5, 7, and 9: K1, yo, knit to marker, sm, work the appropriate row of the Cat's Paw pattern as established in Row 1 to marker, sm, knit to last stitch, yo, k1. (201 sts)

Row 10: Knit.

Next row: K2tog, yo to last st, k1.

BO loosely. Weave in ends. Block to measurements.

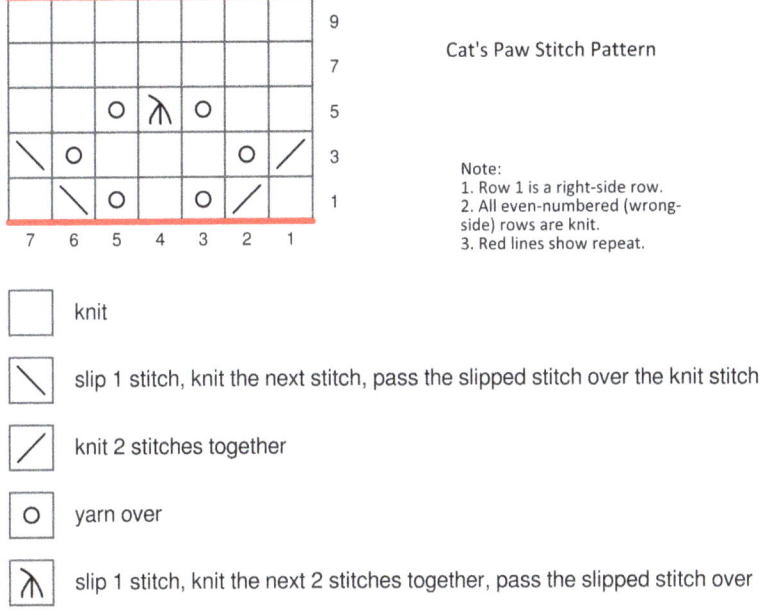

Cat's Paw Stitch Pattern

Note:
1. Row 1 is a right-side row.
2. All even-numbered (wrong-side) rows are knit.
3. Red lines show repeat.

PawPrints – How to Make a Tassel

1. Cut a piece of cardboard (paperboard, card stock) 4 inches (10cm) square.

2. Take a strand of each color, tape the ends to the edge of the card and wrap the strands all the way around the card 20 times.

3. Cut a 12" (30cm) strand and thread tapestry needle with the strand. Run under the yarn at the top of the card (opposite end of the taped strands). Remove needle, tie snugly, and leave ends to later attach to the shawlette.

4. Run scissors under the strands at the other edge of the card, and cut through all strands, as evenly as possible. Remove tape and discard card.

5. Thread tapestry needle with 18" (45cm) of yarn and wrap snugly around tassel 8 times about an inch from the top. Thread tapesty needle with ends and run through the wrap into the inside of the tassel. Cut and bury ends inside.

6. Trim ends of tassel and attach to cast on edge of shawlette, working ends into the first few rows, securely, but making it easy to remove for washing if desired.

Sea Changes Shawl

TRIANGLE SHAWL

From where I knit I am fortunate to have a lovely view of the sea and am fascinated by the changes to its surface throughout the day. This pattern attempts to capture the range of textures – from stormy seas to rippled waves to calm retreating tides. The triangular shawl is knit from the top down, and the simple lace and eyelet stitch patterns that are incorporated into the pattern make for an interesting yet relatively simple knit. Various sizes can be achieved by the number of sections worked. Bind off at the end of Section 1 if you'd like a bandana for a medium-sized dog; at the end of Section 2 if your goal is a shawl for a teen; and continue through Section 3 for a full-sized adult shawl.

Measurements: Wingspan/Length: 52"/130cm
Depth: 25"/62.5cm

Gauge: Blocked: 19 stitches and 32 rows = 4"/10 cm square in Stockinette stitch.
Unblocked: 22 stitches and 32 rows = 4"/10 cm square in Stockinette stitch.

What you'll need:

Miss Babs KEIRA (8oz/225g, 560yds/512m, 100% Superwash Merino Wool: 1 skein Daguerreotype

Size 3 (3.25mm) 32" (80cm) circular needle or size needed to obtain gauge

Stitch marker

Tapestry needle

Sea Changes Shawl

Abbreviations

Pm: place marker
Sm: slip marker
Rm: remove marker
S2kp: slip 2 stitches, 1 at a time, as if to knit. Knit 1 stitch, then pass the 2 slipped stitches over [2 stitches decreased]
Sk2p: slip 1 stitch knitwise to right needle, knit 2 stitches together, then pass slipped stitch over [2 stitches decreased]
Skp: slip 1 stitch knitwise to right-hand needle, knit 1 stitch, then pass slipped stitch over [1 stitch decreased]
Ssk: slip 2 stitches, 1 at a time, as if to knit. Insert left needle into the front of these 2 stitches and knit them together from this position [1 stitch decreased]

Stitch Patterns

Dainty Chevron Stitch Pattern (multiple of 8 stitches + 1)

See Chart.

Row 1 (Wrong Side) and all Wrong Side rows: Purl to end.

Row 2 (Right Side): K1, *ssk, (k1, yo) twice, k1, k2tog, k1; repeat from * to end.

Row 4: Same as Row 2.

Row 6: K1, *yo, ssk, k3, k2tog, yo, k1; repeat from * to end.

Row 8: K1, *k1, yo, ssk, k1, k2tog, yo, k2; repeat from * to end.

Row 10: K1, *k2, yo, s2kp, yo, k3; repeat from * to end.

Repeat Rows 1-10 for pattern.

Simple Chevron Stitch Pattern (multiple of 8 stitches +1)

See Chart.

Row 1 (Right Side): K1, *yo, skp, k3, k2tog, yo, k1, repeat from * to end.

Rows 2 (Wrong Side) and all wrong side rows: Purl to end.

Row 3: K1, *k1, yo, skp, k1, k2tog, yo, k2, repeat from * to end.

Row 5: K1, *k2, yo, sk2p, yo, k3, repeat from * to end.

Row 6: Purl to end.

Repeat Rows 1-6 for pattern.

Roman Stripe Stitch Pattern (multiple of 2 stitches)

Row 1 (Right Side): K1, *yo, k1; repeat from *, end k1.

Row 2 (Wrong Side): K1, *purl; repeat from *, end k1.

Row 3: K1, *k2tog; repeat from *, end k1.

Row 4: K1, *yo, k2tog; repeat from *, end k1.

Row 5: Same as Row 4.

Row 6: Knit to end.

Row 7: Same as Row 6.

Directions

(Begin at center top)

Cast on 3 stitches.

Row 1 (Right Side): (K1, yo) twice, k1. (5 sts)

Rows 2, 4, 6, 8, and 10 (Wrong Side): Purl.

Row 3: (K1, yo) twice, pm, (k1, yo) twice, k1. (9 sts)

Rows 5, 7, 9, and 11: K1, yo, knit to marker, yo, sm, k1, yo, knit to last st, yo, k1. (25 sts)

Section 1

Garter Eyelets

Sea Changes Shawl

Row 1 (Wrong Side): Knit.

Row 2 (Right Side): K1, yo, *k2tog, yo; rep from *to last st before marker, k1, yo, sm, k1, yo, k1, *yo, ssk; rep from* to last st, yo, k1. (29 sts)

Row 3: Knit.

Work the following two rows 6 times (12 rows):

Right Side: K1, yo, knit to marker, yo, sm, k1, yo, knit to last st, yo, k1.

Wrong Side: Purl. (53 sts)

Next row: K1, yo, knit to marker, yo, sm, k1, yo, knit to last st, yo, k1. (57 sts)

Dainty Chevrons

Row 1 and all odd-numbered rows (Wrong Side): Purl.

Row 2: (Right Side): K1, yo, k1, work Row 2 of Dainty Chevron Pattern to last st before marker, k1, yo, sm, k1, yo, k1, work Row 2 of Dainty Chevron Pattern to last 2 sts, k1, yo, k1. (61 sts)

Row 4: K1, yo, k2, work Row 4 of Dainty Chevron Pattern to last 2 sts before marker, k2, yo, sm, k1, yo, k2, work Row 4 of Dainty Chevron Pattern to last 3 sts, k2, yo, k1. (65 sts)

Row 6: K1, yo, k3, work Row 6 of Dainty Chevron Pattern to last 3 sts before marker, k3, yo, sm, k1, yo, k3, work Row 6 of Dainty Chevron Pattern to last 4 sts, k3, yo, k1. (69 sts)

Row 8: K1, yo, k4, work Row 8 of Dainty Chevron Pattern to last 4 sts before marker, k4, yo, sm, k1, yo, k4, work Row 8 of Dainty Chevron Pattern to last 5 sts, k4, yo, k1. (73 sts)

Row 10: K1, yo, k5, work Row 10 of Dainty Chevron Pattern to last 5 sts before marker, k5, yo, sm, k1, yo, k5, work Row 10 of Dainty Chevron Pattern to last 6 sts, k5, yo, k1. (77 sts)

Row 12: K1, yo, k2, work Row 2 of Dainty Chevron Pattern to last

2 sts before marker, k2, yo, sm, k1, yo, k2, work Row 2 of Dainty Chevron Pattern to last 3 sts, k2, yo, k1. (81 sts)

Row 14: K1, yo, k3, work Row 4 of Dainty Chevron Pattern to last 3 sts before marker, k3, yo, sm, k1, yo, k3, work Row 4 of Dainty Chevron Pattern to last 4 sts, k3, yo, k1. (85 sts)

Row 16: K1, yo, k4, work Row 6 of Dainty Chevron Pattern to last 4 sts before marker, k4, yo, sm, k1, yo, k4, work Row 6 of Dainty Chevron Pattern to last 5 sts, k4, yo, k1. (89 sts)

Row 18: K1, yo, k5, work Row 8 of Dainty Chevron Pattern to last 5 sts before marker, k5, yo, sm, k1, yo, k5, work Row 8 of Dainty Chevron Pattern to last 6 sts, k5, yo, k1. (93 sts)

Row 20: K1, yo, k6, work Row 10 of Dainty Chevron Pattern to last 6 sts before marker, k6, yo, sm, k1, yo, k6, work Row 10 of Dainty Chevron Pattern to last 7 sts, k6, yo, k1. (97 sts)

Work the following two rows, twice (4 rows):

Row 1 (Wrong Side): Purl.

Row 2 (Right Side): K1, yo, knit to marker, yo, sm, k1, yo, knit to last st, yo, k1. (105 sts)

Garter Eyelets

Row 1 (Wrong Side): Knit.

Row 2 (Right Side): K1, yo, *k2tog, yo; rep from *to last st before marker, k1, yo, sm, k1, yo, k1, *yo, ssk; rep from* to last st, yo, k1. (109 sts)

Row 3: Knit.

Work the following two rows 3 times (6 rows):

Right Side: K1, yo, knit to marker, yo, sm, k1, yo, knit to last st, yo, k1.

Wrong Side: Purl to end. (121 sts)

Next row: K1, yo, knit to marker, yo, sm, k1, yo, knit to last st, yo, k1. (125 sts)

Sea Changes Shawl

Garter Eyelets

Row 1 (Wrong Side): Knit.

Row 2 (Right Side): K1, yo, *k2tog, yo; rep from *to last st before marker, k1, yo, sm, k1, yo, k1, *yo, ssk; rep from* to last st, yo, k1.

Row 3: Knit. (129 sts)

Work the following two rows, once (2 rows):

Row 1 (Right Side): K1, yo, knit to marker, yo, sm, k1, yo, knit to last st, yo, k1.

Row 2 (Wrong Side): Purl to end. (133 sts)

Simple Chevrons

Row 1 (Right Side): K1, yo, work Row 1 of Simple Chevron Pattern to marker, yo, sm, k1, yo, work Row 1 of Simple Chevron Pattern to last stitch, yo, k1. (137 sts)

Rows 2 (Wrong Side) and all Wrong Side rows: Purl.

Row 3: K1, yo, k1, work Row 3 of Simple Chevron Pattern to last st before marker, k1, yo, sm, k1, yo, k1, work Row 3 of Simple Chevron Pattern to last 2 sts, k1, yo, k1. (141 sts)

Row 5: K1, yo, k2, work Row 5 of Simple Chevron Pattern to last 2 sts before marker, k2, yo, sm, k1, yo, k2, work Row 5 of Simple Chevron Pattern to last 3 sts k2, yo, k1.

Row 6: Purl. (145 sts)

Work the following two rows, once (2 rows):

Row 1 (Right Side): K1, yo, knit to marker, yo, sm, k1, yo, knit to last st, yo, k1.

Row 2 (Wrong Side): Purl. (149 sts)

Roman Stripe

Row 1 (Right Side): K1 yo, k1, work Row 1 of Roman Stripe Pattern to marker, yo, sm, k1, yo, work Row 1 of Roman Stripe Pattern to last 2 sts, k1, yo, k1. (153 sts)

Row 2 (Wrong Side): P3, work Row 2 of Roman Stripe Pattern to 2 sts before marker, p2, sm, p1, work Row 2 of Roman Stripe Pattern to last 3 sts, p3.

Row 3: K1, yo, k2, work Row 3 of Roman Stripe Pattern to last st before marker, k1, yo, sm, k1, yo, k1, work Row 3 of Roman Stripe Pattern to last 3 sts, k2, yo, k1. (157 sts)

Row 4: P4, work Row 4 of Roman Stripe Pattern to 3 sts before marker, p3, sm, p2, work Row 4 of Roman Stripe Pattern to last 4 sts, p4.

Row 5: K1, yo, k3, work Row 5 of Roman Stripe Pattern to 2 sts before marker, k2, yo, sm, k1, yo, k2, work Row 5 of Roman Stripe Pattern to last 4 sts, k3, yo, k1. (161 sts)

Row 6: P5, work Row 6 of Roman Stripe Pattern to 4 sts before marker, p4, sm, p3, work Row 6 of Roman Stripe Pattern to last 5 sts, p5.

Row 7: K1, yo, k4, work Row 7 of Roman Stripe Pattern to 3 sts before marker, k3, yo, sm, k1, yo, k3, work Row 7 of Roman Stripe Pattern to last 5 sts, k4, yo, k1. (165 sts)

End of Section 1.

Work the following two rows, once (2 rows).

Row 1 (Wrong Side): Purl.

Row 2 (Right Side): K1, yo, knit to marker, yo, sm, k1, yo, knit to last st, yo, k1. (169 sts)

Section 2

Repeat Section 1.

End of Section 2. (309 sts)

Sea Changes Shawl

Section 3

Row 1 (Wrong Side): Purl.

Row 2 (Right Side): K1, yo, knit to marker, yo, sm, k1, yo, knit to last st, yo, k1. (313 sts)

Garter Eyelets

Row 1 (Wrong Side): Knit.

Row 2 (Right Side): K1, yo, *k2tog, yo; rep from *to last st before marker, k1, yo, sm, k1, yo, k1, *yo, ssk; rep from* to last st, yo, k1. (317 sts)

Row 3: Knit.

Bind off as follows. Knit the first 2 stitches together through the back loops. Return the single stitch on the right needle to the left needle by slipping it purlwise. Continue until all the stitches are bound off.

Finishing

Weave in ends. Block to measurements, using wires and pins, and stretching just enough to open up the lace patterns, while maintaining the surface texture.

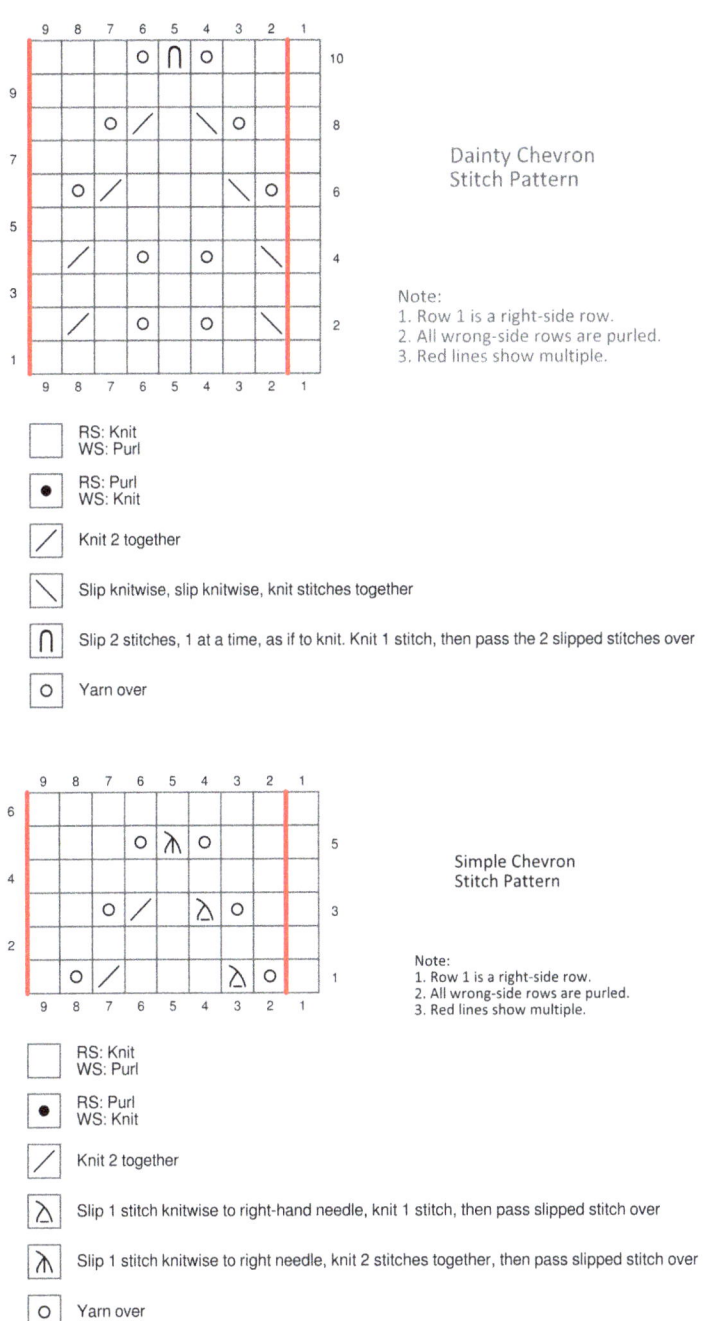

Northern Leaves

TRIANGLE SHAWL

This shawlette is knit from the bottom up, with the triangle shape formed by increases at the beginning and end of right-side rows. A Shetland diamond/leaf stitch pattern and an Estonian diamond/leaf motif are featured. A pink agate pendant from Colombia has been added to the bottom point in this sample.

Measurements: 40 inches across topline x 21 inches from topline to bottom edge / 101.5x53.5cm

Gauge: In Shetland Diamond/Leaf stitch pattern, 18 sts & 36 rows = 4"/10cm.

What you'll need:

Hedgehog Fibres KIDSILK LACE (50g, 420m, 70% Kid Mohair; 30% Silk): 1 skein of Potluck (any colorway in the red/russet range would be a suitable substitute)

US Size 3 (3.25mm) needles or size needed to obtain gauge

US Size 5 (3.75mm) needles (for bind off)

Stitch markers (2)

Tapestry needle

Abbreviations
PM   place marker
SM   slip marker
Skp   slip 1 stitch, knit 1, pass slipped stitch over

Note
The nupp [● on chart] is formed as follows: K1, p1, k1, p1, k1 in the same stitch and pass the last 4 stitches over the first stitch.

Northern Leaves

Cast on 3 stitches.

Knit one row and continue as follows:

Row 1 (RS): K1, yo, k1, yo, k1.

Row 2 (WS) and all wrong-side rows: Knit.

Row 3: K1, yo, k3, yo, k1.

Row 5: K1, yo, k5, yo, k1.

Row 7: K1, yo, k7, yo, k1.

Row 8: Knit. (11 sts)

Note that the shawl shape is created by increasing one stitch at the beginning and end of every right-side row until you have reached a count of 181 stitches, as follows: K1, yo……yo, k1.

Begin pattern

Maintain beginning and ending increases on all right-side rows. Knitting both right- and wrong-side rows,

Work 12 repeats of the Shetland Leaf/Diamond Motif Chart over the center 9 nine stitches as follows:

Row 1 (RS): PM, work Row 1 of the Shetland Leaf/Diamond Motif Chart over the next 9 sts, PM.

Row 2 (WS): Knit.

Row 3: Knit to marker, SM, work the Shetland Leaf/Diamond Motif Chart over the next 9 sts, PM, knit to end.

Row 4: Knit.

Repeat Rows 3 and 4 to complete the 120 rows of the 12 repeats of the Shetland Leaf/Diamond Motif Chart. Remove markers on the final row.

(131 sts)

Maintain beginning and ending increases on all right-side rows. Knitting both right- and wrong-side rows, work the next 38 rows as follows:

Row 1 (RS): K52, PM, work Row 1 of the Estonian Leaf/Diamond Motif Chart over the next 25 sts, PM, k52.

Row 2 (WS): Knit.

Row 3: Knit to marker, SM, work the Estonian Leaf/Diamond Motif Chart over the next 25 sts, SM, knit to end.

Row 4: Knit

Repeat Rows 3 and 4 to complete the 38 rows of the Estonian Leaf/Diamond Motif Chart, removing markers on the last row.

(169 sts)

Maintain beginning and ending increases on all right-side rows. Knitting both right- and wrong-side rows, work the next 10 rows as follows:

Row 1 (RS): K79, PM, work Row 1 of the Shetland Leaf/Diamond Motif Chart over the next 9 sts, PM, k79.

Row 2 (WS): Knit.

Row 3: Knit to marker, SM, work the Shetland Leaf/Diamond Motif Chart over the next 9 sts, SM, knit to end.

Row 4: Knit.

Repeat Rows 3 and 4 for the 10 rows of the Shetland Leaf/Diamond Motif Chart. Remove markers on the final row.

Knit 2 rows. (181sts)

Note: There are no further beginning or ending decreases made from this point.

Knitting both right- and wrong-side rows,

Work 19 multiples of the 9-stitch Shetland Leaf/Diamond Motif Chart across the 181 stitches on your needles as follows:

Northern Leaves

Row 1 (RS): K1, yo, k2tog, k2, PM, work 19 multiples of the 9-stitch Shetland Leaf/Diamond Motif Chart, PM, k2, skp, yo, k1.

Row 2 (WS): Knit.

Repeat these two rows for the 10-row Shetland Leaf/Diamond Motif pattern.

Bind off loosely, on larger needles.

Finishing

Weave in ends. Block to measurements. Thread a tapestry needle with yarn and sew pendant on bottom point, if desired.

Shetland Leaf/Diamond Motif Chart

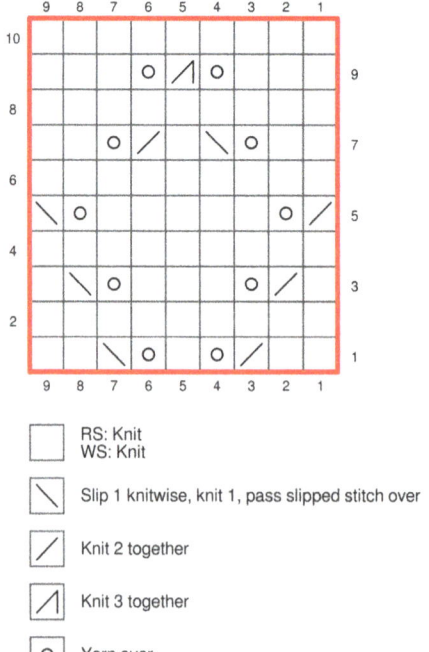

Note

1. Row 1 is a RS row; all odd-numbered rows are worked from right to left.

2. All even-numbered rows are knit.

3. Red lines show multiple and repeat.

4. The black circle symbol is for nupp, which is worked in one stitch.

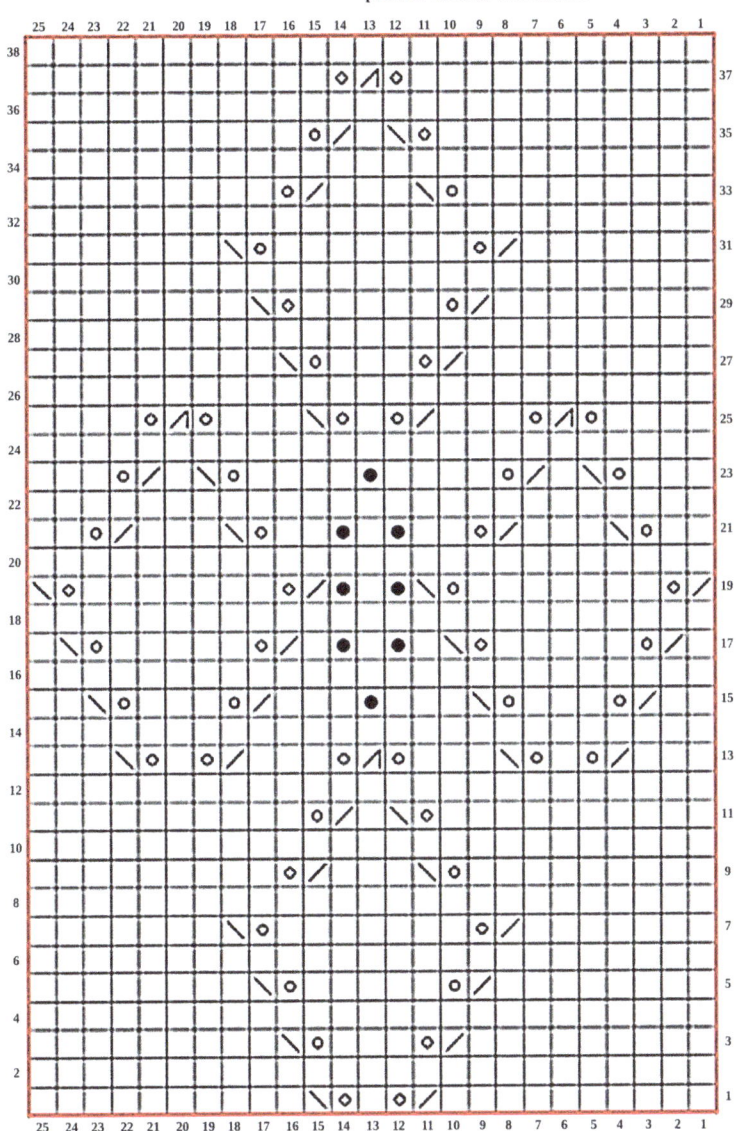

Winter Holiday

TRIANGULAR SHAWL

This long-tailed triangular shawl features knit-purl texture, eyelet lace, and mosaic stitch patterns in three colors of Cascade 220 Sport. Knit from the top down, the design incorporates seasonal snowflakes and holiday candy canes – and an optional pendant.

Measurements: Topline: 55"/140cm.
Topline to bottom point: 20"/51cm

Gauge: In Knit-Purl Texture, 22 sts and 32 rows = 4"/10cm.
In Eyelet Lace, 22 sts and 32 rows = 4"/10cm.
In Mosaic Grill, 24 sts and 44 rows = 4"/10cm

What you'll need:

Cascade Yarns CASCADE 220 SPORT (50g, 150m/164 yards, 100% Peruvian Highland Wool): 1 skein each of #9451 Lake Chelan Heather (Color A), #8401 Silver Grey (Color B), and #9404 Ruby (Color C)

US Size 5 (3.75mm) 32" (80cm) circular needle or size needed to obtain gauge

Stitch marker

Tapestry needle

Abbreviations
PM   place marker
SM   slip marker
RM   remove marker
k2tog   knit 2 stitches together
skp   slip 1 stitch knitwise, knit the next stitch,
              pass the slipped stitch over
s2kp   slip 2 stitches knitwise, knit the next stitch,

Winter Holiday

	pass the slipped stitches over
sl	slip the stitch
pfb	purl in front and back of the stitch
p2tog	purl two stitches together
yo	yarn over
wyib	hold yarn at back of work
wyif	hold yarn at front of work

Designer Note

If you choose to work swatches, please re-use the yarn to ensure that you have enough for the entire project. The pattern was designed to use most of the yarn in the three skeins.

Cast on 3 stitches with color A.

Setup (continue with color A)

Row 1 (RS): K1, yo, k1, yo, k1. (5 sts)

Rows 2, 4, and 6 (WS): Purl.

Row 3: (K1, yo) 4 times; k1. (9 stitches)

Row 5: (K1, yo) twice; k2, yo, PM, k1, yo, knit to last 2 sts (yo, k1) twice. (15 sts)

Section 1 – Knit-Purl Texture 1

Row 1 (RS): (K1, yo) twice; *(k1, p1) rep from * to 1 st before marker, k1, yo, SM, k1, yo, *(k1, p1) rep to last 3 sts, k1, (yo, k1) twice.

Row 2 (WS): Purl.

Row 3: (K1, yo) twice; *(p1, k1) rep from * to marker, yo, SM, k1, yo, *(k1, p1) rep to last 2 sts, (yo, k1) twice.

Row 4: Purl.

Repeat Rows 1-4 until you have 87 stitches, ending with a WS row.

Change to Color B.

Row 1 (RS): (K1, yo) twice; knit to marker, yo, SM, k1, yo, knit to last 2 sts, (yo, k1) twice. (93 sts)

Row 2 (WS): Purl.

Change back to Color A.

Row 3: (K1, yo) twice; knit to marker, yo, SM, k1, yo, knit to last 2 sts, (yo, k1) twice. (99 sts)

Row 4: Purl.

Cut yarn.

Section 2 – Snowflake Eyelets

Snowflake Eyelet Stitch Pattern (multiple of 8 sts; 6-row repeat)

See chart.

Row 1 (RS): *(K3, skp, yo, k1, yo, k2tog), rep from *.

Rows 2 (WS) and all other WS rows: Purl.

Row 3: *(K4, yo, S2kp, yo, k1), rep from *.

Row 5: Repeat Row 1.

Change back to Color B.

Row 1 (RS): (K1, yo) twice; knit to marker, yo, SM, k1, yo, knit to last 2 sts, (yo, k1) twice. (105 sts)

Row 2 (WS) and all WS rows: Purl.

Row 3: (K1, yo) twice; work Row 1 of Snowflake Eyelet pattern 6 times, k2, yo, SM, k1, yo, work Row 1 of Snowflake Eyelet pattern 6 times, k2, (yo, k1) twice. (111 sts)

Row 5: (K1, yo) twice; k2, work Row 3 of Snowflake Eyelet pattern 6 times, k3, yo, SM, k1, yo, k1, work Row 3 of Snowflake Eyelet pattern 6 times, k4, (yo, k1) twice. (117 sts)

Row 7: (K1, yo) twice; k4, work Row 5 of Snowflake Eyelet pattern

Winter Holiday

6 times, k4, yo, SM, k1, yo, k2, work Row 5 of Snowflake Eyelet pattern 6 times, k6, (yo, k1) twice. (123 sts)

Row 9: (K1, yo) twice; knit to marker, yo, SM, k1, yo, knit to last 2 sts, (yo, k1) twice. (129 sts)

Row 10: Purl.

Change to Color C.

Row 11: (K1, yo) twice; knit to marker, yo, SM, k1, yo, knit to last 2 sts, (yo, k1) twice. (135 sts)

Row 12: Purl.

Change back to Color B.

Row 13: (K1, yo) twice; knit to marker, yo, SM, k1, yo, knit to last 2 sts, (yo, k1) twice. (141 sts)

Row 14: Purl.

Section 3 – Mosaic Grill 1

Row 1 (RS) (Color C): (K1, yo) twice; knit to marker, yo, SM, k1, yo, knit to last 2 sts, (yo, k1) twice. (147 sts)

Row 2 (WS) (Color C): Purl, increasing 12 sts evenly across row, using pfb technique. (159 sts)

Row 3 (Color B): (K1, yo) twice; (k2, sk1 wyib) 25 times, k2, yo, SM, k1, yo, (k2, sl1 wyib) 25 times, k2, (yo, k1) twice. (165 sts)

Row 4 (Color B): P5, k1, sl1 wyif, (k2, sl1 wyif) 24 times, k1, p5, k1, sl1 wyif, (k2, sl1 wyif) 24 times, k1, p5.

Row 5 (Color C): (K1, yo) twice; knit to marker, yo, SM, k1, yo, knit to last 2 sts, (yo, k1) twice. (171 sts)

Row 6 (Color C): Purl.

Row 7 (Color B): (K1, yo) twice; k1, (k2, sk1 wyib) 27 times, k1, yo, SM, k1, yo, k1, sl1 wyib, (k2, sk1 wyib) 26 times, k3, (yo, k1) twice. (177 sts)

Row 8 (Color B): P6, k1, sl1 wyif, (k2, sl1 wyif) 26 times, k1, p3, k1, sl1 wyif, (k2, sl1 wyif) 26 times, k1, p6.

Row 9 (Color C): (K1, yo) twice; knit to marker, yo, SM, k1, yo, knit to last 2 sts, (yo, k1) twice. (183 sts)

Row 10 (Color C): Purl.

Cut Color B yarn.

Change to Color A:

Row 11: (K1, yo) twice; knit to marker, yo, SM, k1, yo, knit to last 2 sts, (yo, k1) twice. (189 sts)

Row 12: Purl, decreasing 12 sts evenly across row, using p2tog technique. (177 sts)

Change back to Color C:

Row 13: (K1, yo) twice; knit to marker, yo, SM, k1, yo, knit to last 2 sts, (yo, k1) twice. (183 sts)

Row 14: Purl.

Cut Color C yarn.

Change back to Color A.

Row 15: (K1, yo) twice; knit to marker, yo, SM, k1, yo, knit to last 2 sts, (yo, k1) twice. (189 sts)

Row 16: Purl

Section 4 – Knit-Purl Texture 2

Continue with Color A.

Row 1 (RS): (K1, yo) twice; *(p1, k1) rep from * to marker, yo, SM, k1, yo, *(k1, p1) rep to last 2 sts, (yo, k1) twice.

Row 2 (WS): Purl.

Row 3: (K1, yo) twice; *(k1, p1) rep from * to 1 st before marker,

Winter Holiday

k1, yo, SM, k1, yo, *(k1, p1) rep to last 3 sts, k1, (yo, k1) twice.

Row 4: Purl.

Repeat Rows 1-4 until you have 237 stitches, ending with a WS row.

Row 1 (RS): (K1, yo) twice; knit to marker, yo, SM, k1, yo, knit to last 2 sts, (yo, k1) twice. (243 sts)

Row 2 (WS): Purl.

Change to Color B.

Row 3: (K1, yo) twice; knit to marker, yo, SM, k1, yo, knit to last 2 sts, (yo, k1) twice. (249 sts)

Row 4: Purl.

Change back to Color A.

Row 1 (RS): (K1, yo) twice; knit to marker, yo, SM, k1, yo, knit to last 2 sts, (yo, k1) twice. (255 sts)

Row 2 (WS): Purl, increasing 20 sts evenly across row, using pfb technique. (275 sts)

Cut yarn.

Section 5 – Mosaic Grill 2

Row 1 (RS) (Color B): (K1, yo) twice; knit to marker, yo, SM, k1, yo, knit to last 2 sts, (yo, k1) twice. (281 sts)

Row 2 (WS) (Color B): Purl.

Row 3 (Color C): (K1, yo) twice; k1, sl1 wyib, (k2, sk1 wyib) 45 times, k1, yo, SM, k1, yo, k1, sl1 wyib, (k2, sk1 wyib) 45 times, k1, (yo, k1) twice. (287 sts)

Row 4 (Color C): P4, k1, sl1 wyif, (k2, sl1 wyif) 45 times, k1, p3, k1, sl1 wyif, (k2, sl1 wyif) 45 times, k1, p4.

Row 5 (Color B): (K1, yo) twice; knit to marker, yo, SM, k1, yo, knit to last 2 sts, (yo, k1) twice. (293 sts)

Row 6 (Color B): Purl.

Row 7 (Color C): (K1, yo) twice; (k2, sk1 wyib) 47 times, k3, yo, SM, k1, yo, k1, (k2, sk1 wyib) 47 times, k2, (yo, k1) twice. (299 sts)

Row 8 (Color C): P5, k1, sl1 wyif, (k2, sl1 wyif) 46 times, k1, p7, k1, sl1 wyif, (k2, sl1 wyif) 46 times, k1, p5.

Row 9 (Color B): (K1, yo) twice; knit to marker, yo, SM, k1, yo, knit to last 2 sts, (yo, k1) twice. (305 sts)

Row 10 (Color B): Purl, decreasing 20 sts evenly across row, using p2tog technique. (285 sts)

Change back to Color C.

Row 11: (K1, yo) twice; knit to marker, yo, SM, k1, yo, knit to last 2 sts, (yo, k1) twice. (291 sts)

Row 12: Purl.

Change back to Color B.

Row 13: (K1, yo) twice; knit to marker, yo, SM, k1, yo, knit to last 2 sts, (yo, k1) twice. (297 sts)

Row 14: Purl.

Cut yarn.

Section 6 – Candy Cane Eyelets

Candy Cane Eyelet Stitch Pattern (multiple of 8 sts; 12-row repeat)

See chart.

Row 1 (RS): *K1, skp, yo, k1, yo, k2tog, k2; rep from*.

Row 2 (WS) and all other WS rows: Purl.

Row 3: *Skp, yo, k3, yo, k2tog, k1; rep from *.

Row 5: *K3, skp, yo, k3; rep from *.

Winter Holiday

Row 7: *K2, skp, yo, k4; rep from *.

Row 9: *K1, skp, yo, k5; rep from *.

Row 11: *Skp, yo, k6; rep from *.

Change to Color C.

Row 1 (RS): (K1, yo) twice; knit to marker, yo, SM, k1, yo, knit to last 2 sts, (yo, k1) twice. (303 sts)

Row 2 (WS) and all WS rows: Purl.

Row 3: (K1, yo) twice; k3, work Row 1 of Candy Cane Eyelet pattern 18 times, k2, yo, SM, k1, yo, k3, work Row 1 of Candy Cane Eyelet pattern 18 times, k2, (yo, k1) twice. (309 sts)

Row 5: (K1, yo) twice, k5, work Row 3 of Candy Cane pattern 18 times, k3, yo, SM, k1, yo, k4, work Row 3 of Candy Cane pattern 18 times, k4, (yo, k1) twice. (315 sts)

Row 7: (K1, yo) twice; k7, work Row 5 of Candy Cane pattern 18 times, k4, yo, SM, k1, yo, k5, work Row 5 of Candy Cane pattern 18 times, k6, (yo, k1) twice. (321 sts)

Row 9: (K1, yo) twice; k9, work Row 7 of Candy Cane pattern 18 times, k5, yo, SM, k1, yo, k6, work Row 7 of Candy Cane pattern 18 times, k8, (yo, k1) twice. (327 sts)

Row 11: (K1, yo) twice; k11, work Row 9 of Candy Cane pattern 18 times, k6, yo, SM, k1, yo, k7, work Row 9 of Candy Cane pattern 18 times, k10, (yo, k1) twice. (333 sts)

Row 13: (K1, yo) twice; k13, work Row 11 of Candy Cane pattern 18 times, k7, yo, SM, k1, yo, k8, work Row 11 of Candy Cane pattern 18 times, k12, (yo, k1) twice. (339 sts)

Row 14: Purl.

Change to Color B.

Row 1 (RS): (K1, yo) twice; knit to marker, yo, SM, k1, yo, knit to last 2 sts, (yo, k1) twice. (345 sts)

Row 2 (WS): Purl.

Row 3: (K1, yo) twice; knit to marker, yo, RM, k1, yo, knit to last 2 sts, (yo, k1) twice. (351 sts)

Row 4: Knit.

Row 5 (no increases): *K2tog, yo; rep from * to last st, k1.

Bind off using a stretchy bind-off technique, such as the Russian Bind Off, as follows: Knit 2 sts, *slip the 2 sts back to the left needle, knit the 2 sts together through the back loops, knit 1 st, rep from *.

Weave in ends. Block to measurements.

Note
1. Row 1 is a right-side row.
2. All even-numbered (wrong-side) rows are purled.
3. Red lines show multiple.

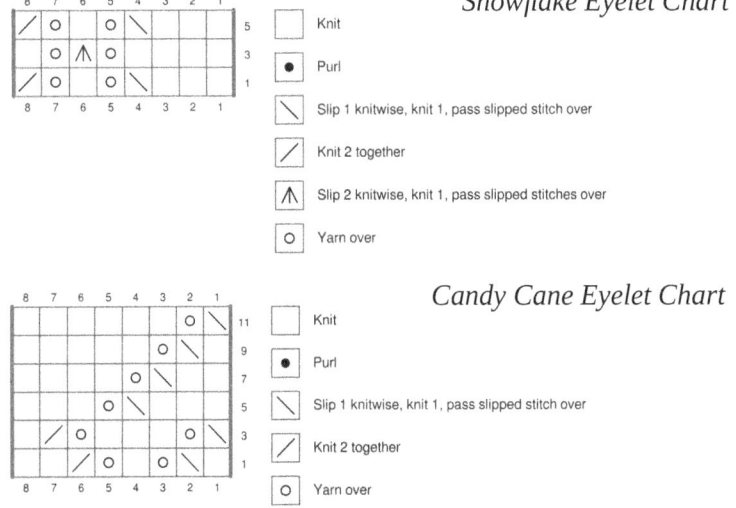

Snowflake Eyelet Chart

Candy Cane Eyelet Chart

Estonian Colorwork Cowl

COLORWORK COWL

This double-wrap cowl features an old Estonian motif I have adapted from a black and white chart I found on a visit to a thrift shop in Tallinn – the capital of Estonia. The accessory is knit in seven colorways of Alice Starmore's Hebridean 2-ply (fingering-weight) yarn.

Measurements: Circumference: 48"/122cm
Height: 7.5"/19cm

Gauge: In stranded colorwork stitch pattern, 28 sts & 33 rounds = 4"/10cm

What you'll need:

Alice Starmore HEBRIDEAN 2-Ply (0.88oz/25g, 93yds/85m, 100% Wool): 1 ball each of Erica (Color A); Pebble Beach (Color B); Clover (Color C); Driftwood (Color D); Lapwing (Color E); Kittiwake (Color F); and Machair (Color G)

US size 3 (3.25mm) 32 inch/80cm circular knitting needle (or size needed to obtain gauge)

Stitch marker

Tapestry needle

Cast on 340 stitches in Color A. Join in the round, placing a stitch marker to indicate beginning of round.

Work 5 multiples of the 31 rounds of the Estonian Colorwork – Chart 1 on the 340 stitches.

Work 5 multiples of the 30 rounds of the Estonian Colorwork – Chart 2 on the 340 stitches.

BO loosely in Color A. Weave in ends and block to measurements.

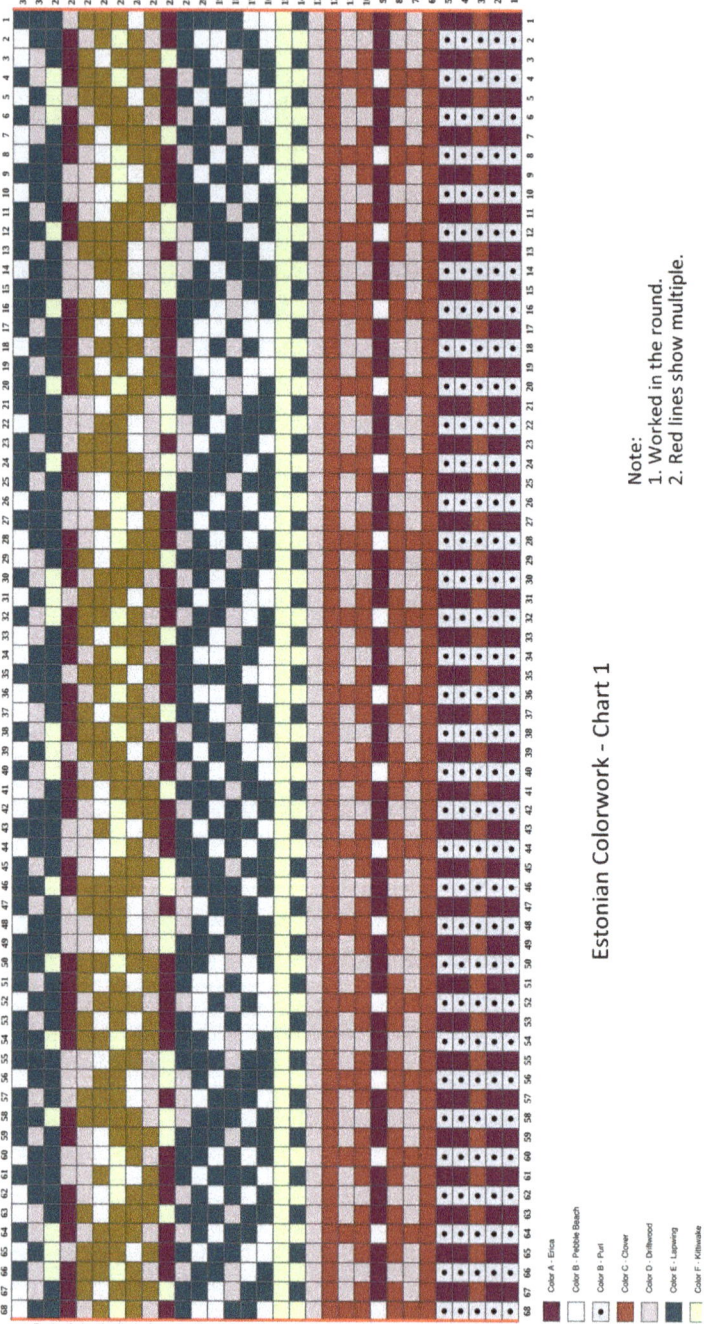

Estonian Colorwork - Chart 2

Note:
1. Worked in the round.
2. Red lines show multiple.

www.ingramcontent.com/pod-product-compliance
Lightning Source LLC
Chambersburg PA
CBHW040417100526
44588CB00022B/2859